EMMANUEL JOSEPH

Knowledge for Analyzing Business Achievements For Expansion

Copyright © 2025 by Emmanuel Joseph

All rights reserved. No part of this publication may be reproduced, stored or transmitted in any form or by any means, electronic, mechanical, photocopying, recording, scanning, or otherwise without written permission from the publisher. It is illegal to copy this book, post it to a website, or distribute it by any other means without permission.

First edition

This book was professionally typeset on Reedsy.
Find out more at reedsy.com

Contents

1. Chapter 1: Understanding the Business Landscape — 1
2. Chapter 2: Identifying Core Competencies and Capabilities — 3
3. Chapter 3: Conducting SWOT Analysis — 5
4. Chapter 4: Financial Analysis and Forecasting — 7
5. Chapter 5: Market Research and Customer Insights — 9
6. Chapter 6: Competitive Analysis and Positioning — 11
7. Chapter 7: Strategic Planning and Goal Setting — 13
8. Chapter 8: Operational Efficiency and Process Improvement — 15
9. Chapter 9: Risk Management and Mitigation — 17
10. Chapter 10: Innovation and Adaptability — 19
11. Chapter 11: Building a Strong Organizational Culture — 21
12. Chapter 12: Measuring Success and Continuous Improvement — 23

1

Chapter 1: Understanding the Business Landscape

The business landscape is constantly shifting, influenced by factors such as technological advancements, economic fluctuations, and changing consumer behaviors. For businesses to thrive, they must stay informed and adaptable. This requires a deep understanding of the external environment, including market trends, regulatory changes, and competitive dynamics. By keeping a finger on the pulse of these elements, businesses can anticipate challenges and capitalize on opportunities. It's essential to conduct regular market analysis to identify emerging trends and potential disruptors that could impact the business.

Additionally, businesses must recognize the importance of a holistic approach to understanding the landscape. This means not only focusing on immediate competitors but also considering broader industry developments. For instance, technological innovations in one sector can have ripple effects across multiple industries. Businesses that are aware of these interconnections can better prepare for the future. Furthermore, understanding the global market is crucial, as economic conditions in one region can influence operations and opportunities in another.

Another key aspect of understanding the business landscape is acknowledging the role of social and cultural shifts. Consumer preferences and societal values are evolving, and businesses must stay attuned to these changes. For example, the growing emphasis on sustainability and ethical practices is reshaping industries. Companies that align their strategies with these values can build stronger connections with their customers and enhance their brand reputation. This requires continuous monitoring of societal trends and adapting business practices accordingly.

Finally, businesses should leverage data and analytics to gain deeper insights into the business landscape. Advanced analytics tools can help identify patterns and trends that might not be immediately apparent. By harnessing the power of data, businesses can make more informed decisions and develop strategies that are responsive to the ever-changing environment. In essence, understanding the business landscape is an ongoing process that requires vigilance, adaptability, and a willingness to embrace change.

2

Chapter 2: Identifying Core Competencies and Capabilities

Identifying and leveraging core competencies is fundamental to a business's success. Core competencies are the unique strengths that differentiate a company from its competitors and form the basis of its competitive advantage. These can include specialized knowledge, advanced technology, strong customer relationships, or exceptional talent. By focusing on these areas, businesses can create value for their customers and build a sustainable market position.

To identify core competencies, businesses must conduct a thorough internal analysis. This involves evaluating various aspects of the organization, including resources, processes, and performance. It's important to recognize that core competencies are not static; they evolve over time as the business grows and the market changes. Therefore, businesses should regularly reassess their strengths and make strategic investments to enhance and protect these capabilities.

Once core competencies are identified, businesses must effectively leverage them to gain a competitive edge. This requires aligning business strategies with these strengths. For example, a company with a strong research and development (R&D) capability should prioritize innovation and invest in new product development. Similarly, a business known for excellent customer service should focus on enhancing customer experiences and building long-term relationships. By capitalizing on core competencies, businesses can differentiate themselves and create unique value propositions.

Moreover, businesses should consider how to enhance their core competencies through partnerships and collaborations. Strategic alliances with other companies, research institutions, or industry experts can provide access to additional resources and knowledge. These collaborations can help businesses strengthen their capabilities and stay ahead of the competition. Ultimately, identifying and leveraging core competencies requires a strategic approach, continuous evaluation, and a commitment to excellence.

3

Chapter 3: Conducting SWOT Analysis

A SWOT analysis is a strategic tool used to evaluate a business's internal and external environment. It stands for Strengths, Weaknesses, Opportunities, and Threats. This analysis provides a comprehensive view of the factors that can influence a business's success and helps in developing effective strategies. By systematically assessing these elements, businesses can make informed decisions and take proactive steps to achieve their goals.

Strengths and weaknesses are internal factors that reflect the business's capabilities and limitations. Strengths are the positive attributes that give the business a competitive edge, such as a strong brand, skilled workforce, or advanced technology. Weaknesses, on the other hand, are areas that need improvement, such as limited resources, outdated processes, or lack of expertise. Identifying these factors allows businesses to build on their strengths and address their weaknesses to enhance overall performance.

Opportunities and threats are external factors that can impact the business. Opportunities are favorable conditions that the business can capitalize on, such as emerging markets, technological advancements, or changing consumer preferences. Threats, conversely, are challenges that could hinder the business's progress, such as economic downturns, competitive pressures, or regulatory changes. By recognizing these external factors, businesses can develop strategies to seize opportunities and mitigate threats.

Conducting a SWOT analysis is an iterative process that requires regular review and updates. The business environment is constantly changing, and new strengths, weaknesses, opportunities, and threats may emerge over time. Therefore, businesses should incorporate SWOT analysis into their strategic planning process and use it as a guide for decision-making. By maintaining a dynamic SWOT analysis, businesses can stay agile and responsive to the evolving landscape.

4

Chapter 4: Financial Analysis and Forecasting

F inancial analysis is a critical component of business strategy, providing insights into a company's financial health and performance. It involves examining key financial metrics such as revenue, expenses, profitability, and cash flow. By analyzing historical financial data, businesses can identify trends and assess their financial stability. This analysis is essential for making informed decisions, allocating resources effectively, and planning for the future.

One of the primary goals of financial analysis is to evaluate the business's profitability. This involves analyzing income statements to understand revenue sources, cost structures, and profit margins. Businesses can identify areas where they can reduce costs or increase revenue to improve profitability. Additionally, understanding cash flow is crucial for ensuring that the business has enough liquidity to meet its obligations and invest in growth opportunities.

Forecasting is another important aspect of financial analysis. By creating financial forecasts, businesses can set realistic goals and plan for future growth. Forecasting involves projecting future revenue, expenses, and cash flow based on historical data and market trends. This helps businesses anticipate potential challenges and identify opportunities for expansion.

Accurate forecasting enables businesses to make strategic investments and allocate resources efficiently.

Effective financial management also involves monitoring key performance indicators (KPIs) and comparing them against industry benchmarks. This provides a clear picture of how the business is performing relative to its peers. By tracking KPIs, businesses can identify areas where they are excelling and areas that need improvement. Regular financial analysis and forecasting enable businesses to stay on track, make data-driven decisions, and achieve their strategic objectives.

5

Chapter 5: Market Research and Customer Insights

Market research is essential for understanding customer needs, preferences, and behaviors. By gathering and analyzing data, businesses can gain valuable insights into target markets and customer segments. This information guides product development, marketing strategies, and customer service initiatives. By staying attuned to customer feedback and market trends, businesses can adapt to changing demands and build strong, loyal relationships with their audience.

One of the key components of market research is identifying target markets. This involves segmenting the market based on demographic, geographic, psychographic, and behavioral factors. By understanding the characteristics of different customer segments, businesses can tailor their products and services to meet their specific needs. This targeted approach increases the likelihood of customer satisfaction and loyalty.

Customer insights are derived from various sources, including surveys, focus groups, social media, and transaction data. Analyzing this data helps businesses understand customer preferences, pain points, and purchasing behaviors. For example, businesses can use customer feedback to identify areas for improvement and develop new products that address unmet needs. Additionally, understanding customer behavior helps businesses optimize their marketing efforts and enhance customer experiences.

Furthermore, businesses should continuously monitor market trends and competitive dynamics to stay relevant. Market trends provide valuable information about emerging opportunities and potential threats. By keeping a close eye on the market, businesses can adjust their strategies to remain competitive. Additionally, understanding the competitive landscape helps businesses identify their unique value proposition and differentiate themselves from competitors. Effective market research and customer insights are critical for making informed decisions and achieving long-term success.

6

Chapter 6: Competitive Analysis and Positioning

Competitive analysis is a crucial aspect of business strategy, enabling businesses to understand their competitors and develop effective positioning strategies. This analysis involves evaluating competitors' strengths, weaknesses, strategies, and market share. By identifying gaps and opportunities, businesses can develop unique value propositions and differentiate themselves in the market. Effective positioning communicates the benefits of a company's products or services, creating a compelling reason for customers to choose them over competitors.

One of the first steps in competitive analysis is identifying key competitors. This involves researching companies that operate in the same market and offer similar products or services. By understanding who the competitors are, businesses can evaluate their market position and identify areas for improvement. Additionally, analyzing competitors' strategies and tactics provides valuable insights into industry best practices and emerging trends.

Positioning is about creating a distinct image in the minds of customers. This involves defining the unique benefits and attributes of a company's products or services and communicating them effectively. Businesses must identify their unique selling points (USPs) and highlight them in their marketing efforts. For example, a company that offers eco-friendly products can position itself as a leader in sustainability, appealing to environmentally conscious customers. Effective positioning helps businesses stand out in a crowded market and build a strong brand identity.

Furthermore, businesses should continuously monitor competitors and adjust their strategies accordingly. The competitive landscape is dynamic, and businesses must stay agile to remain relevant. Regularly conducting competitive analysis ensures that businesses are aware of new entrants, emerging threats, and changing market conditions. By staying informed and proactive, businesses can maintain their competitive edge and achieve long-term success.

7

Chapter 7: Strategic Planning and Goal Setting

Strategic planning is the process of defining a company's long-term objectives and determining the actions needed to achieve them. This involves setting a clear vision and mission, followed by establishing specific, measurable, achievable, relevant, and time-bound (SMART) goals. Strategic planning provides Strategic planning provides a roadmap for the business, ensuring that all efforts are aligned with the company's overall vision. It involves assessing the internal and external environment, setting long-term objectives, and developing action plans to achieve those goals. This process encourages a forward-thinking mindset and helps businesses anticipate future challenges and opportunities. By having a clear strategic plan, businesses can allocate resources effectively and prioritize initiatives that drive growth and success.

Goal setting is a critical component of strategic planning. SMART goals provide a clear framework for what the business aims to achieve and how it will measure success. These goals should be specific, meaning they are clearly defined and unambiguous. They should be measurable, allowing progress to be tracked and evaluated. Achievable goals are realistic and attainable, considering the resources and constraints of the business. Relevant goals align with the company's overall strategy and mission. Finally, time-bound goals have a defined timeframe for completion, creating a sense of urgency and accountability.

Effective strategic planning and goal setting require input from various stakeholders within the organization. This collaborative approach ensures that different perspectives are considered and that the plan is comprehensive. Regularly reviewing and adjusting the strategic plan is also essential, as it allows businesses to stay responsive to changing market conditions and internal developments. By fostering a culture of strategic thinking and continuous improvement, businesses can achieve their long-term objectives and maintain a competitive edge.

In summary, strategic planning and goal setting are fundamental to business success. They provide direction, focus, and a framework for measuring progress. By aligning efforts with the company's vision and mission, businesses can achieve sustainable growth and create value for their stakeholders. Regularly revisiting and refining the strategic plan ensures that it remains relevant and effective in an ever-changing environment.

8

Chapter 8: Operational Efficiency and Process Improvement

Operational efficiency is key to maximizing productivity and minimizing costs. Businesses must continually evaluate and optimize their processes to eliminate waste, reduce redundancies, and improve performance. Implementing best practices, leveraging technology, and fostering a culture of continuous improvement contribute to operational excellence. By streamlining operations, businesses can deliver higher quality products and services, enhancing customer satisfaction and profitability.

One of the first steps in achieving operational efficiency is mapping out existing processes and identifying areas for improvement. This involves analyzing workflows, identifying bottlenecks, and assessing the overall effectiveness of operations. By understanding how current processes work, businesses can pinpoint inefficiencies and develop strategies to address them. This may include redesigning workflows, automating repetitive tasks, or reallocating resources to more critical areas.

Technology plays a crucial role in enhancing operational efficiency. By adopting innovative tools and systems, businesses can streamline processes, improve communication, and increase productivity. For example, enterprise resource planning (ERP) systems integrate various business functions, providing real-time visibility into operations and facilitating better decision-making. Similarly, customer relationship management (CRM) systems help businesses manage customer interactions and improve service delivery. Embracing technology not only improves efficiency but also enables businesses to stay competitive in a rapidly evolving market.

Fostering a culture of continuous improvement is essential for sustaining operational excellence. This involves encouraging employees to identify and address inefficiencies, promoting collaboration, and providing ongoing training and development. By empowering employees to take ownership of process improvement, businesses can create a dynamic and responsive work environment. Additionally, regularly reviewing and updating processes ensures that they remain effective and aligned with the company's strategic objectives. In conclusion, operational efficiency and process improvement are critical for achieving long-term success. By continuously evaluating and optimizing operations, businesses can enhance productivity, reduce costs, and deliver superior products and services to their customers.

9

Chapter 9: Risk Management and Mitigation

Every business faces risks, both internal and external. Effective risk management involves identifying, assessing, and mitigating potential threats. This process includes developing contingency plans, implementing controls, and monitoring risk factors. By proactively managing risks, businesses can minimize their impact and ensure continuity. A robust risk management strategy protects the company's assets, reputation, and long-term viability.

Identifying risks is the first step in the risk management process. This involves conducting a thorough assessment of the internal and external environment to identify potential threats. Internal risks may include operational inefficiencies, financial mismanagement, or employee-related issues. External risks can range from economic downturns and market volatility to natural disasters and regulatory changes. By understanding the full spectrum of risks, businesses can develop comprehensive strategies to address them.

Once risks are identified, they must be assessed in terms of their likelihood and potential impact. This involves evaluating the probability of each risk occurring and the extent of its consequences. Risk assessment helps businesses prioritize their efforts and allocate resources effectively. For example, high-probability, high-impact risks may require immediate attention and robust mitigation measures, while low-probability, low-impact risks can be monitored and managed with less intensive efforts.

Mitigating risks involves implementing strategies and controls to reduce their likelihood and impact. This may include developing contingency plans, diversifying investments, or enhancing security measures. Businesses should also establish clear communication channels and protocols for responding to risk events. Regularly reviewing and updating risk management strategies ensures that they remain effective and aligned with the company's evolving needs. By adopting a proactive approach to risk management, businesses can safeguard their assets, reputation, and long-term success.

In summary, risk management is an essential component of business strategy. By identifying, assessing, and mitigating potential threats, businesses can minimize their impact and ensure continuity. A robust risk management strategy provides a framework for responding to challenges and protecting the company's interests. Regularly reviewing and updating risk management practices ensures that businesses remain resilient and adaptable in a constantly changing environment.

10

Chapter 10: Innovation and Adaptability

Innovation is essential for staying competitive and relevant in a fast-paced market. Businesses must foster a culture that encourages creativity, experimentation, and continuous learning. By embracing new technologies, processes, and ideas, companies can drive innovation and differentiate themselves. Adaptability is equally important, as it allows businesses to respond quickly to changes in the market, customer needs, and industry trends. A willingness to innovate and adapt is crucial for long-term success.

Creating a culture of innovation starts with leadership. Business leaders must set the tone by promoting a vision that values creativity and supports risk-taking. This involves providing employees with the resources and autonomy to explore new ideas and experiment with different approaches. Recognizing and rewarding innovative efforts also reinforces a culture of continuous improvement and encourages employees to contribute their best ideas.

Embracing new technologies is a key driver of innovation. Businesses should stay informed about technological advancements and assess their potential impact on operations, products, and services. For example, adopting artificial intelligence (AI) and machine learning can enhance data analysis, improve customer experiences, and streamline processes. Similarly, leveraging the Internet of Things (IoT) can enable real-time monitoring and optimization of operations. By integrating cutting-edge technologies, businesses can stay ahead of the curve and maintain a competitive edge.

Adaptability requires businesses to be agile and responsive to change. This involves regularly monitoring market trends, customer feedback, and industry developments to identify emerging opportunities and threats. Businesses should be prepared to pivot their strategies and operations as needed to stay relevant. For example, during the COVID-19 pandemic, many businesses quickly adapted to remote work, e-commerce, and digital marketing to continue serving their customers. Being adaptable also means learning from failures and setbacks, using them as opportunities for growth and improvement.

In conclusion, innovation and adaptability are critical for long-term business success. By fostering a culture of creativity and continuous learning, embracing new technologies, and staying agile in the face of change, businesses can thrive in a dynamic market. A commitment to innovation and adaptability ensures that companies remain relevant, competitive, and positioned for growth.

11

Chapter 11: Building a Strong Organizational Culture

A positive organizational culture is the foundation of a successful business. It influences employee engagement, productivity, and retention. Businesses must cultivate a culture that aligns with their values, mission, and goals. This involves fostering open communication, promoting collaboration, and recognizing and rewarding achievements. A strong culture attracts top talent, enhances employee satisfaction, and drives overall business performance.

Building a strong organizational culture starts with clearly defining the company's values and mission. These principles serve as the guiding framework for all business activities and decisions. Leaders play a crucial role in exemplifying these values and setting the tone for the organization. By consistently demonstrating the desired behaviors and attitudes, leaders can inspire employees to embrace and embody the company's culture.

Open communication is essential for creating a positive work environment. Businesses should encourage transparency and provide channels for employees to share their ideas, concerns, and feedback. Regular team meetings, town halls, and one-on-one sessions can facilitate open dialogue and ensure that employees feel heard and valued. Effective communication also involves actively listening to employees and addressing their needs and concerns in a timely manner.

Promoting collaboration and teamwork is another key aspect of a strong organizational culture. Businesses should create opportunities for employees to work together, share knowledge, and support one another. This can be achieved through cross-functional projects, team-building activities, and collaborative technologies. By fostering a sense of community and mutual support, businesses can enhance employee engagement and productivity.

In summary, building a strong organizational culture requires a deliberate and ongoing effort. By defining and exemplifying the company's values, fostering open communication, and promoting collaboration, businesses can create a positive work environment that supports employee engagement and performance. A strong culture not only attracts top talent but also drives overall business success.

12

Chapter 12: Measuring Success and Continuous Improvement

Measuring success involves tracking key performance indicators (KPIs) and analyzing results to determine whether business goals are being met. By regularly reviewing performance data, businesses can identify areas for improvement and make data-driven decisions. Continuous improvement is an ongoing process that involves setting new targets, implementing changes, and monitoring progress. By striving for excellence and learning from both successes and failures, businesses can achieve sustained growth and success.

KPIs are critical metrics that reflect the performance and health of the business. These indicators can include financial metrics such as revenue growth, profit margins, and return on investment, as well as operational metrics like customer satisfaction, employee engagement, and process efficiency. By tracking KPIs By tracking KPIs, businesses can gain valuable insights into their performance and identify trends over time. This data-driven approach allows businesses to make informed decisions and prioritize areas that need attention. For example, if customer satisfaction scores are declining, businesses can investigate the underlying causes and take corrective actions to improve the customer experience. Similarly, if employee engagement metrics are low, businesses can implement initiatives to boost morale and motivation. Regularly monitoring KPIs ensures that businesses stay on track and achieve their strategic objectives.

Continuous improvement is an integral part of measuring success. This involves regularly assessing processes, identifying areas for enhancement, and implementing changes to achieve better outcomes. Businesses should foster a culture of continuous improvement, where employees are encouraged to suggest and implement improvements. This proactive approach not only enhances operational efficiency but also drives innovation and competitiveness. By continually striving for excellence, businesses can adapt to changing market conditions and stay ahead of the competition.

Implementing a continuous improvement process requires a systematic approach. This involves setting clear improvement goals, developing action plans, and monitoring progress. Businesses should use tools such as Six Sigma, Lean, and Total Quality Management (TQM) to streamline processes and eliminate inefficiencies. By regularly reviewing and refining processes, businesses can achieve higher levels of performance and quality. Additionally, continuous improvement efforts should be aligned with the company's strategic objectives to ensure that they contribute to overall success.

In conclusion, measuring success and continuous improvement are essential for achieving long-term business success. By tracking KPIs and analyzing performance data, businesses can make informed decisions and identify areas for enhancement. Fostering a culture of continuous improvement encourages innovation and operational excellence. By consistently striving for better outcomes, businesses can achieve sustained growth, stay competitive, and create value for their stakeholders.

www.ingramcontent.com/pod-product-compliance
Lightning Source LLC
LaVergne TN
LVHW020743090526
838202LV00057BA/6209